The opposite of evil is peace.

Truly Medieval—and Modern

Comments by

Richard Simon Hanson

Paul Swehla, moved by perceptive intuition has here woven together two dissimilar traditions: that of Medieval Jewish mysticism and the classic Nordic story of Peer Gynt, developing the theme of redemption. Early on in this development, redemption proceeds out of situations of guilt and shame—though guilt and shame, which may exhibit the same symptoms, are not the same. One may realize shame without guilt or guilt without shame.

The author was introduced to the thought world of Kabbalah (often transliterated as Cabala) by a Jewish master through whom he learned the terms that he lists in a helpful glossary. The reader would also do well to first read through the text of Ibsen's drama of *Peer Gynt*. Though he almost adopted the persona of Peer Gynt as he set out, the content that follows is really an explanation of Kabbalah, a movement that arose and expanded following the half millennium period of Talmud Torah in both its versions—that of the Babylonian and the Jerusalem Talmud.

> Jewish people who live in Upper Galilee honor a second century teacher named Shim'on Bar Yochai as the founder whose gravesite is on the north side of a ravine between the ruins of ancient Khirbet Shema and contemporary Meiron, but the final flowering of the movement was led by Isaac Luria, whose gravesite is in nearby Tsefet. Luria was a contemporary of the Germans' Martin Luther.

It is not surprising to this reviewer that he finds kinship of thought with Carl Jung. His concept of "soul," a fluid word with various meanings, is truly Medieval—and modern! In Biblical Hebrew, the word nefesh is customarily translated as "soul" but really designates the individual breath of any creature.

In summary, much of this treatise is an introduction to the thought world of Kabbalah, classically an adventurous intellectual movement of Medieval Judaism.

Among other gems in the text is this line: always, there is a future, and forever, there is hope.

Dr. Richard Simon Hanson
Ph.D. Harvard, 1963
Professor Emeritus of Religion and Biblical Hebrew
Luther College
Decorah, Iowa

GILGUL

TRANSMIGRATION

by

Paul Swehla

TIKKUN
PUBLISHING
P.O. Box 51
Decorah, IA 52101

EAN: 978-1535018401
ISBN: 1535018402

Tikkun Publishing
P.O. Box 51
Decorah, IA 52101

Printed by CreateSpace, an Amazon.com Company

Dedication

In dedication to all the unborn: from the spilled seed to the discharged embryo; from the aborted fetus to the miscarried and the stillborn; to all the souls that were forced to wait for their opportunity to repair our broken world.

I deeply regret that the publication of this text is a disappointment to my father and mother. I pray, however, that it is not construed as a dishonor, heaven forbid! For this is neither my intention nor does this kind of spite reside in my heart. It is for this reason, as irony and paradox will have it, that I dedicate this book in honor of my parents, with respect and reverence.

In memory of my friend Ryan, and my sister, Tonya.

Contents

Book Two: Revelation

Book Three: Redemption

PREFACE

At Peace with Paradox

Gilgul began as an outgrowth from an ongoing philosophical correspondence I'd been having with a friend and mentor of mine. Our letters and emails eventually resulted in my writing a short theosophical novel, originally entitled *Sketches of a Transmigrant Soul*. Rooted in Kabbalistic philosophy and Judeo-Christian theology, the story is loosely based on Henrick Ibsen's character and phantasmagorical play by the same name, Peer Gynt.

Peer Gynt is reincarnate. In his various incarnate forms, he tries—albeit paradoxically and at times unwillingly—to overcome the transgressions from his past lives in order to redeem his soul. Over the millennia, and throughout repeated incarnations, Peer learns that he must play his part—as we all must do—in Tikkun Olam, the cosmic restoration of our broken, fallen world.

For the sake of background and context, much of the original text digressed into technical Kabbalistic detail. While relevant, these teachings weighed down Peer's narrative and poetry. When my friend read the early manuscripts, he recommended that I rewrite *Sketches* from prose into verse. The result is *Gilgul: Transmigration*.

While the epic poetry of Peer's story can be readily understood on the surface through context and deduction, there are many technical terms and concepts that draw directly from traditional Judaism and Jewish Kabbalah. In order to accommodate the reader, I've provided the Introduction that follows this Preface, a Glossary of Terms and a bibliographical list of recommended reading (these last two can be found at the end of the book). I recommend that the uninitiated reader, after reading the Introduction, take a few minutes to read through the Glossary prior to embarking upon Peer's narrative poetry.

*   *   *

I wrote *Sketches* and *Gilgul* after serving more than a decade in federal prison. It is said that there is irreversible psychological damage that occurs after seven years of imprisonment; I personally have no doubt about this. My sentence was linked to my best friend's overdose and death, and I was exhausted from wrestling with the guilt, shame and remorse, self pity, humiliation and dread. Years of profound soul searching and introspection had created a deep void within me. I'd lost all of my appeals, my wife and son, my sister, and—like Michael Stipe of REM—my religion as well. With another decade in prison ahead of me, this was a very dark night for my soul.

I was a disillusioned Christian; in fact, I'd all but defected. For years I had lead a small Messianic congregation, teaching Messianic Judaism and the Hebraic roots of Christianity. I taught much of the deeper historical and contextual background behind Judeo-Christianity. We celebrated all of the biblical festivals like Shabbat, Pesach, and the High Holidays. I taught introductory Hebrew and linguistics related to traditional rabbinical interpretation of the scriptures. We observed many of the mitzvot and ceremonial laws. In short, I fully taught the observance of Torah for believers in Yeshua (Jesus) as the Jewish and Gentile Messiah—or what might otherwise be referred to as Jewish Christianity.

But Justice must ultimately be balanced by Mercy; the Law must be tempered by Grace. This truth is firmly rooted within both Jewish and Christian theology. Likewise, this is fundamental to Kabbalah. Indeed, the mystery of Torah is revealed through Grace. In the end, peace lies at the root of paradox.

I came to the heretical conclusion that all interpretation is subjective and fallible. I was disgusted by the absolute refusal of our religious elders, leaders and teachers—historically and presently—to admit with humility that they simply do not have the answers to life's questions of inequity and suffering. In my not-so-humble opinion, dogma and doctrine belonged in the realm of hypocrisy. So I waged a sustained polemical war on those who would dictate how one ought to live her life without first walking a mile in her shoes—which of course is utterly impossible, not to mention hypocritical on my part.

My struggle was futile. I held these judges in contempt while trying to refrain from dictating how my students should live their

Paul Swehla

lives. An existential crisis began to unfold. As my evolving beliefs increasingly rejected traditional interpretation as fundamentally flawed, I simultaneously relinquished many of the doctrines which serve as the very foundation of Christian and Jewish theology. Further, I forfeited the ordination vested in me by my immediate elders, leaders, and teachers. Quite simply, I'd become an apostate. Thus, I held myself in contempt. Enter paradox.

This is a difficult position to be in, but in the end, I came to believe that before anyone can truly teach, lead or guide, he or she must experience, first hand, such an existential crisis. To arrive at this incongruent and cognitively dissonant reality is to cancel and deny oneself. While mankind is innately good, all sin and fall short of the glory of G-d. Moreover, this revelation that good and evil coincide is a deeply disturbing psychological concept. To exacerbate this, there are no rational answers to questions of suffering, salvation, life after death, or heaven and hell.

Thus, the existential questions come into bold relief. Who am I? Why am I here? Who am I to judge? No one can truly know anyone else's suffering, let alone the deeply intimate life experiences that make them precisely the person they are. Interpretation, at this point, becomes irrelevant and infinitely subjective; any subsequent dictum by any elder, teacher, or leader becomes insulting and dehumanizing.

This becomes either the starting point for teaching, leading, and instruction, or the ending point of hypocrisy. Do unto others as you would have them do unto you. Judge not lest ye be judged. Remove the log from your own eye before trying to remove the sliver from your brother's eye. Here I was, again, back where I'd started at the Torah, or the Law. Justice.

Such paradox required a Kierkegaardian leap of faith. Having deemed myself unfit, impure and unholy, I renounced my ordination and abandoned my congregation.

I was just finishing my bachelor's degree through correspondence in theology and Judaic studies. I'd spent years studying traditional Judaism in tandem with evangelical Christianity. This, coupled with the existential philosophy and theologies of Kierkegaard, Hegel, Buber, Heschel, Niebuhr and Tillich, set the stage for the mystical. And so it was at this time that I dove head first into Lurianic Kabbalah.

By the time I enrolled into my school's graduate program in theology, I had written *Sketches* and was in the process of writing *Gilgul*. I proposed my thesis with these works as my foundation: Not only was Jesus a Jew to the very essence of his being, he was an existentialist, a mystic and a master of Kabbalah. Further, I would defend my argument that Jesus taught, or at least never ruled out the possibility of, reincarnation. In short, Jesus was a proto-Chasidic Rebbe.

Needless to say, my proposed thesis was denied. I was deemed a heretic, an apostate, and I withdrew from the graduate program.

Yet my friend and mentor was adamant: "Besides the mystics, most people don't realize religion can be personalized, largely because of the various religions' take it or leave it attitude."

So I began to study Buddhist philosophy (disregarding its cosmology) along with the writings of Carl Jung. I began to regularly practice seated meditation, harmonizing the eastern religious and spiritual experience with western and Greco-Roman ideology. It was here where I began to find peace within my paradox. It should be noted that it is absolutely essential that the mystic remain rooted in the physical. One of the best ways to accomplish this is through our labor—and our suffering—both of which, incidentally, may be likened to birth and death. Our work largely defines the meaning and purpose in our lives, and suffering gives us something to rise above; that is, hope.

With that said, I'm grateful for my occupation during this time as an instructor in my institution's culinary arts program. Not only had this experience been supremely enriching on many levels, but the work kept me anchored in the real world. I have no doubt that this daily routine and mundane discipline ensured my sanity as I ascended through ethereal spiritual realms and descended into the abysmal dark night of the soul.

There are some who refer to Kabbalah as Hinduism with a kippa. So be it. Still, it was this full immersion into the absolute darkness that paradoxically revealed the Divine Light that dispels it. I shed the meaningless trappings of my existence, letting go of a lifetime of

Paul Swehla

guilt and shame. Call it an existential leap of faith, a journey, a quest; call it any one of these, or all of the above.

Always, there is a future, and forever, there is hope. I emerged from this darkness not necessarily a changed person, but as a sort of new creation, an ever changing work in progress with newfound hope and courage. Having received the revelation that I have the power to face and repair the brokeness in my life and that which I had caused in the lives of others, I could now change, grow, and in effect, achieve some semblance of redemption in the here and now.

So without further ado, I present to you my "thesis" that never was. For better or worse, my name is Peer Gynt, and I am reincarnate. And we are at peace with paradox.

Paul Swehla

Acknowledgments

Special thanks to my teacher, Rabbi Yonassan Gershom, for his meticulous research and publication of *Jewish Tales of Reincarnation*. Without him, this present work would have been impossible.

Thanks also to my friend and editor, Bruce Larson, who remained loyal and never abandoned me, unlike so many who have. Thanks to my friend Carl Homstad, who inspired and encouraged me to write these poems, and to Mick Layden for his cover design. Special thanks to my friend Randy Scheel, who believed in me in spite of my dark moods, and Jeff Hussinger for his help, direction and advice with editing and proof reading this book.

Finally, thanks to Philip Glass, Henryk Gorecki, Arvo Pärt, J. S. Bach, Edvard Grieg and all the others whose music helped to cultivate my inspiration in the mystical; and to the artist formerly known as Robert Zimmerman whose music kept me grounded—and sane—rooted in the mundane.

Paul Swehla

INTRODUCTION

Traditionally, a transmigrant soul doesn't usually tell her own story. Tales of reincarnation are typically told in the third person narrative. Veiled allusions, often coupled with "a secret word to the wise," are used to clue the initiate into the esoteric teachings of Kabbalah. By its very nature, the story has a deeper meaning. These midrashic, parabolic tales are meant to convey profound spiritual truths about forgiveness, redemption, freedom, and responsibility.

Every soul is held accountable to the Creator of the universe, blessed be He. Perhaps the most important element of these stories is the Jewish concept of Tikkun, and by extension, Tikkun Olam, the systematic process of universal reconfiguration. While Tikkun means "repair," it generally refers to the reparation of the human soul, and Tikkun Olam literally entails the restoration and reparation of our broken, fallen world. These reparations are made possible through Gilgul, from the abbreviated Hebrew phrase, gilgul neshamot, meaning reincarnation of the soul. Transmigration.

So we learn from our mistakes. But this is not the moral of the story. Reincarnation provides a way for the soul to play its part in Tikkun Olam. For when a soul returns to the earth plane, it does so in order to complete unfinished business. Similar to a quest, the soul must accomplish one or more specific good deeds or commandments known in Hebrew as Mitzvot (sing. Mitzvah). A soul's failure in a past life to perform or adhere to certain Mitzvot—based upon the moral and ethical teachings of Torah—often results in the consequential suffering of reincarnation.

For example, when someone dies, the soul goes before a heavenly tribunal known as a beit din (Hebrew for "house of judgment"). Upon review, with Satan acting as the prosecuting attorney, if the soul has failed to play her part in the elevation of the universal consciousness, she is returned to the earth plane again and again, until the required mitzvot are accomplished. Only then are redemption and restoration of the soul attained, ultimately extending to the universe as a whole.

And so we turn, turn, turn. We do Teshuva, we repent and change our ways. We repair the brokenness of our lives. We begin to understand that our decisions are weighed in the balance, each affecting their respective cosmic consequence. Like it or not, every soul carries with it the burden of responsibility: we either draw our universe deeper into darkness or we elevate it to its eventual and inevitable restoration and redemption, and the dawning of the Messianic Age. Meanwhile, every decision made, every action taken or neglected, bears with it a consequence—either degrading or restoring our world and universe. It is our soul that serves as the medium of exchange in this cosmic economy balanced by justice and mercy—in very much the same way that the Law must be balanced by Grace.

Generally, a soul is unable to remember the events of her past lives. However, this knowledge can be revealed through prayer and meditation, through visions, dreams, and mystical visitations. Often, Eliyahu ha Navi—Elijah the Prophet—appears. Other times, the medium is impregnated by another soul called an Ibbur which attaches itself to the human body for the sake of communication with or teaching of another.

Peer Gynt is often confronted by an Ibbur either in the form of the Button Moulder or through the soul of a Tzaddik (a holy and righteous person who acts as a guide to lost souls), a rabbi or some other teacher.

At one point, Peer's soul refuses to go before the Beit Din for judgment. Disembodied, his soul wanders, possessing the bodies and controlling the behavior of both humans and animals. In this state his soul is unredeemable, for as a Dybbuk, the limits of evil are inexhaustible. Yet even through all of this, there is still redemption.

In the Beginning

Bereshit bara Elohim et hashamayim v'et ha aretz—In the beginning, G-d created the heavens and the earth. So the Bible teaches us this truth.

Likewise, Kabbalah teaches that the end is embedded in the beginning in the same way that the beginning is embedded in the

Paul Swehla

end—like the flames of a burning coal. The same is true of the Hebrew "aleph-beit," understood as the protoplasm, the building blocks of creation. Indeed, the Aleph is embbeded in the Tav—like the Greek Alpha and the Omega—and thus, the beginning is embedded in the end.

In the beginning—before G-d created the heavens and the earth—there was a concept, a word—the Word, if you will. This concept was Adam Kadmon, the primordial man. All of creation emanates from Adam Kadmon, including, of course, Adam and Eve who were created in the image of G-d. All souls originate from Adam Kadmon.

Put another way, Adam Kadmon represents the light of the world. This light passes from the Ein Soph, the Infinite One, to be evenly suffused throughout the worlds, or universes, of Emanation, Creation, Formation and Action. However, during the process of creation, certain vessels called Sephirot, intended to contain this holy light, were shattered into sparks, called Nitzotzot. These Nitzotzot fell to the lower, darker realms of consciousness here in the material world.

Peer Gynt is one of these sparks.

The Doctrine of Soul Roots

There is a midrashic tale that helps to explain the kabbalistic doctrine of soul roots. The Talmud, Midrash, and Zohar teach us that when Cain killed his brother Abel, their parents, Adam and Eve, in an attempt to prevent further bloodshed, decided to refrain from sexual intercourse. One hundred and thirty years later, Cain is killed by Lamech, and Adam and Eve reconvene with their love-making. Seth is conceived and born.

However, during the time when Adam and Eve separated themselves from each other, Adam took to satisfying himself through masturbation. The souls in Adam's seed were, in effect, bastardized during ejaculation. These souls expected to enter the womb of mother Eve, but instead, Adam spilled his seed on the ground. The souls were lost and had to wait to be born at a later time. To complicate matters, the impure thoughts that accompanied Adams's act became an inherent part of these souls in need of redemption.

Peer Gynt is one of these souls.

Further, despite the fact that Abel doesn't have any physical descendants as a result of being murdered by Cain, we can nevertheless speak of a soul descending from the root of Abel. This teaching is the basis, in part, for the Doctrine of Soul Roots. Those souls that were destined to come down through the soul of Abel were eventually reconceived and born vicariously through Seth.

Peer Gynt is not one of these souls.

Creation, Revelation, and Redemption

All of being and creation can be arranged as if it were three acts of a play. The psychologist and teacher of Kabbalah, Gabriella Samuel, correctly compares these three acts of our play to the dialectical philosophy of G.F.W. Hegel's thesis, anti-thesis, and synthesis.

So, Act One of Creation, known in Hebrew as Tzimtzum, is Hegel's thesis. Act Two is The Fall, or Shevirat ha Kelim, perhaps better understood as man's first intimate exposure to and knowledge of good and evil after eating the forbidden fruit from the selfsame tree. This is Hegel's antithesis which we can simply refer to as revelation. Act Three is restoration and redemption, or Tikkun and synthesis.

The Ein Soph, or Infinite One, throughout all of creation is omnipotent, existing everywhere. However, this aspect of G-d cannot be fully fathomed by humankind. Still, before G-d created the universes, nothing beyond the Ein Soph existed. We can envision the Ein Soph as the infinite source of Divine Light of the world, pure energy, bound by neither time nor space. A will to create arose within the Ein Soph. Thus began Act One of our drama, a very technical process known in Lurianic Kaballah as Tzimtzum, literally, contraction, condensation, or concealment.

During Tzimtzum, the Infinite created within itself an empty void in order to construct the finite worlds of existence. This primordial

Paul Swehla

void was infused by a single beam of Divine Light which was harnessed in a manner so as not to annihilate any physical substance it would otherwise create. The empty space then converted to Kelim, or vessels, comprising the Ten Sephirot, whose purpose was to receive the Ohr Ein Soph, the Light of the Divine.

The Kelim, that is, the Ten Sephirot, collectively constitute the primordial human, Adam Kadmon—the Tree of Life. Adam Kadmon serves as the conduit for this creative energy, and all of creation emanates from him to the Ten Sephirot. From these archetypal energies, these emanations of the Sephirot, innumerable finite worlds or universes have been created, including those four that are known.

The universe of Asiyah is the physical world of Action. Yetzirah is the universe of Creation, where angels reside. Beriyah is the universe of Formation, where souls are created. Lastly, there is the universe of Atzilut, or the world of Emanation and the origin of the Ten Sephirot.

There is actually a fifth universe, revealed to us as Adam Kadmon, sometimes referred to as the Tree of Life. This world is inaccessible; yet it is the source and root of all souls. Adam Kadmon is the source of all creation, in closest proximity to the Ein Soph. All five universes have a direct correlation to the five levels of the soul, discussed below.

In the intitial processes of creation, known as Tohu (Chaos), the Kelim were able to receive the Divine Light; however, they were unable to transmit. As a result, the upper Three Sephirot (known as the Three Mothers, Aleph, Mem, and Shin) were damaged, and the lower seven were destroyed. This is the Fall, Hegel's anti-thesis, the second act of our divine drama, known in Kabbalah as Shevirat ha Kelim, literally, "the shattering of the vessels." The broken shards of these lower Seven Sephirot, known as Klippot, fell to the lowest of the four worlds, Assiyah, our physical universe. Here, the Klippot have taken on material substance.

The Klippot are inherently evil and variously referred to as shells, coverings, or garments. These outer layers conceal the Nitzotzot, or Divine Sparks, hidden inside. Indeed, before we're able to reach the flesh of the fruit or enjoy the savory fulfillment of a nut, we must first peel away the bitter skin or crack the hard shell. So too must the evil and unholiness be removed from the physical in order to access the Holy Sparks of Divinity residing within each of us.

The objective, then, is to elevate the Divine Sparks of creation back to their original source. This is done in the world of Action through the performance of good deeds, acts of charity, and kindness, through prayer, meditation, and the observance of G-d's commandments— known collectively as Mitzvot. Thus, we arrive at the third act of our drama—synthesis—or Tikkun, restoration, and redemption.

The Nitzotzot must be redeemed and restored. The process of Tikkun begins in the higher realms where the upper three Sephirot, in spite of having been damaged, are able to reconstruct the lower seven. These lower seven are reconstructed into Partzufim. Gabriella Samuel calls this a gestalt-like archetypal configuration of faces that are able to harness and direct the sparks back to their source. Now with an ability to both give and receive the Divine Light without being destroyed as before, balance is achieved through harmonious equilibrium. The physical world is then rooted simultaneously with the world of the lower Seven Sephirot.

Meanwhile, in order to initiate this process in the physical world, Adam and Eve were created. In the image of G-d, this "lower Adam" (Adam means "man" in Hebrew) was formed in the likeness of the primordial human Adam Kadmon, with the intent for him to make reparations to this broken universe. Instead, man brought about his own demise, the fall and exile from the ideal state of Gan Eden, the Garden of Eden, or Paradise.

In a world mixed with good and evil, where the Divine Sparks remain hidden among the broken shards, our mission is to elevate the sparks through Mitzvot. In this manner we repair our broken world through Tikkun, helping souls to return to their roots in Adam Kadmon. Thesis, anti-thesis, and synthesis—creation, revelation and redemption. Ultimately, the restoration of our broken world will culminate with the coming of the Messiah and the ushering in of the Olam Haba, the World to Come.

Paul Swehla

The Five Levels of the Soul

We cannot begin to understand Tikkun or Gilgul without considering the anatomy of a soul. It is important to understand that there are five levels of the human soul. These five levels directly correspond to the five universes discussed above. In addition, as Gabriella Samuel points out, the five levels of the soul can be viewed as a kind of developmental psychology.

Ascending from the lowest level of the soul, we begin with Nephesh, corresponding to the material world and the universe of Asiyah-Action. Nephesh is united with the seed, the embryo and the fetus; it develops from gestation through birth, life and death. The Nephesh resides in the physical vessel, be it human, plant, animal or any other element of the created world. While the Nephesh originates in the Klippot, it is not in itself inherently evil; however, the Nephesh inclines towards the Yetzer Hara, the evil inclination. Dominated by physical desire, emotion, base natural instincts and the pursuit of pleasure, the Nephesh serves as the foundation for the higher levels of the soul.

The second level of the soul, bound to the Nephesh, is the Ruach, or the "middle spirit," and corresponds to the universe of Yetzirah-Formation. Developmentally, the Ruach grows and matures like an infant nursing at her mother's breast. The Ruach enjoys the freedom to "go up and down" (Eccl. 3:21) within the spiritual realms. The Ruach is often translated as the "breath of life." It can be likened to the heart of one's personality and the animating force of individuality. The Ruach, together with the Nephesh, elevate and support the third level of the soul, the Neshamah, the G-dly "upper soul."

The Neshamah corresponds to the universe of Beriyah-Creation. It is here where the mind develops, including deeper levels of spiritual and intellectual precognition. The Neshamah level of the soul navigates the prophetic and dream states, the body simultaneously bound to the Divine—"simulspaceously"—able to move freely between the two. The Neshamah is literally a part of G-d and serves as the vehicle which elevates the lower soul from the realm of the Yetzer Hara towards the Yetzer ha Tov, the good inclination. It is important to note that the Neshamah is inherently good and perfect in and of itself. Hence it is referred to as the "G-dly soul."

These first three levels of the soul—Nephesh, Ruach, and Neshamah—all reside within the human body. They can be compared to the psychology of the human personality, namely instinct, emotion, and intellect. Likewise, they correlate to the blood, "for life is in the blood" (Lev. 11:17), the heart and the brain.

Chayah, the fourth level of the soul, corresponds to the universe of Atzilut-Emanation. The Chayah level of the soul does not permanently reside with the body. Rather, Chayah surrounds the body and connects with all other souls to their root, into what the psychologist Carl Jung referred to as the "collective unconsciousness." The Chayah level of the soul is the conduit through which supernatural communication can occur from one soul to another. Chayah can be accessed to tap information from the past, present, and future.

The fifth and highest level of the soul is known as Yechida and corresponds to the highest supernal realm of Adam Kadmon. Yechida, unlike the other four levels of the soul, does not accompany the body. Yechida is closest in proximity to the Ein Soph and the Source of Creation. It generates energy from the Nitzotzot, the Divine Sparks that constitute the soul. The Yechida level of the soul accounts for the rare and unexplainable ability for some to transcend beyond space and time in order to perform miracles.

A Poem: Bereshit—In the Beginning

I. Tzimtzum: Creation

> The empty and infinite self yields to the finite
> Infused into the primordial void by a single beam of light
> Concealed and constricted
> Like Leviathan in the abysmal night
> So as not to annihilate this something from nothing

Vessels: Kelim holding light
Eyes, nose, ears, and mouth of the primordial man
Adam Kadmon, in the fifth world above—root of the soul

II. Shevirat ha Kelim: Revelation

The beginning is embedded in the end
Like the flames of a burning coal
Three wounded mothers give birth
To seven faces without fear
Destroyed at delivery by the infinite light
Injected into their shattered countenances
Shells are cracked to release the nut
As bitter skin is peeled away
Exposing revelatory flesh of fruit   .
Where sparks of the divine are hidden inside
The vessels shatter and break
They fall through the lower realms of the Tetragrammaton
The four worlds below Adam Kadmon:

Atzilut—Emanation: Ten Sephirot
Beriyah—Formation: Where souls are born
Yetzirah—Creation: Where angels reside
Asiyah—Action: Material, you and I

III. Tikkun: Redemption

Nut within the shell, fruit beneath the skin
Conquered for the flesh within

Remove unholiness, evil, and sin
Extracting light from the physical realm
Tikkun, redemption, and reconfiguration:
Mitzvot, good deeds, divine restoration
Kindness, prayer, and meditation
Seven faces reappear as the upper three repair
Lower seven reconstruct the damage done below:
Light conducting, ebb and flow, balance is achieved

Another world, one and the same
Adam and Eve, the image of G-d, kavananah
Intent to repair, elevate the flame
Tikkun Olam, repair our broken world
All souls return to Adam Kadmon
When all is restored
Mashiach will come to usher in Olam Haba
And the World to Come

Jewish and Gentile Themes in *Gilgul*

I would be remiss if I failed to address the prevailing Jewish themes that surface and recur throughout *Gilgul*. Some of these are very dark and obscure, and certainly, many readers will be unfamiliar with some of the references made in Peer Gynt's poetry. Again, I refer these readers to the glossary in the back; I suggest that a few minutes be set aside to read through the entries prior to embarking upon Peer Gynt's quest.

Aside from this, the foremost element in need of attention is the significance of Peer Gynt's revelation that he is Jewish. This realization directly links him to a cosmological scheme in line with the traditional conceptualization and purpose of Torah in his life, and by extension, to all of creation. In this sense, he becomes aware of and begins to

Paul Swehla

comprehend the significance of his past reincarnations in relation to his obligation as a Jew. Peer Gynt carries the weight of the world upon his shoulders. Indeed, it is the duty of all Jews to ultimately and collectively pave the way for the redemption of the world.

This obligation is a direct result of the marriage that took place between the Creator of the universe, blessed be He, and Israel at Mount Sinai. Every single Jewish soul was present at this ceremony, consecrated through a Ketuvah (ritual marriage contract) and through the giving and receiving of Torah. Peer Gynt's soul was present for this ceremony. He took the vows with all of the other Yiddische Neshamot: "Na'aseh v'nishmah—We will hear and obey all that Adonai has spoken." All Jewish souls are bound in covenant to and collectively constitute the bride of YHVH through Torah.

Thus, the Jews' raison d'etre is summed in the Sh'ma, the quintessential statement of faith and wedding vow (cf. Dt. 6:4–9; 11:13–21; Num. 15:37–41; Mt. 23:37–40; Mk. 12:29–31). Even Jesus correctly ruled that this is the greatest mitzvah of all: "Hear, O Israel, the L-RD our G-d, the L-RD is One." The entire Torah can be summed in this one commandment—and all Jews are bound by the covenant of Torah in its entirety.

It is important to note that Jewish identity is confirmed through the mother (or through strict conversion to Judaism, in which case Kabbalah teaches that such a convert is actually a lost Jewish soul returning to the covenant via Teshuva and Gilgul). Thus, Aase's apostasy, assimilation and conversion to Christianity doesn't change the fact that her son, Peer, is still Jewish, or more accurately, a Yiddische Neshamah—a Jewish soul. Nor does this change Aase or Peer's obligation as Jews to perform Teshuva, to turn and repent, to return to the ways of Adonai: to observe the Mitzvot of Torah and thereby play their parts in Tikkun Olam.

Lest some become jealous or confused—or even violent, heaven forbid!—this is not to suggest that the gentiles and Christians of the world are relieved of their responsibility to play their parts in Tikkun Olam. Indeed, all souls find their root in Adam Kadmon. Moreover, all souls—Jew and Gentile—are bound by Torah. Even Jesus said, "Do not think that I have come to abolish Torah..." (Mt. 5:17). After all, in the beginning was the word and the word became flesh.

Nevertheless, suffice it to say that as far as gentiles are concerned with the covenant of Torah, a place in Olam Haba is redeemed vicariously through grace. For "the mystery of Torah is revealed through grace!"

Still, messianic conceptions and misconceptions muddy the theologocial waters. We need to look no further than the horrors of the Inquisition, the pogroms, blood libels and the Holocaust to prove this point. Yet again, gentiles have a place in Olam Haba. In fact, some schools of Jewish thought recognize two distinct manifestations of the Mashiach who will redeem Israel and the world. The first is Mashiach ben David—Messiah, son of David—prophesied to come and reign as king of Israel and the world. The other is Mashiach ben Yoseph—Messiah, son of Joseph, the suffering servant, also king of Israel and the world. The Jews await the advent of the former while Christians recognize prophesy fulfilled through the latter.

Touché. And so the beginning is embedded in the end; the aleph with the tav; the alpha and the omega.

Closing Remarks

It has been difficult for me to refrain from delving more deeply into the context and background, the deeper significance of how the multifaceted traditional Jewish elements provide an exquisite tapestry to Peer's narrative poetry; this is beyond the scope of this introduction (although many will no doubt feel that I've already breached this scope). The reason I rewrote the prose of *Sketches* into the verse of *Gilgul* in the first place was to lighten the technical Jewish and Kabbalistic load.

Finally, the uninformed reader, whether Jew or Gentile, must read between the lines. To quote Jesus again, "he who has ears, let him hear" (Mt. 11:15). So I present you with Peer Gynt's story—a parabolic midrash as a "secret word to the wise." May we all recall the significance of *teshuva*, to turn and return—through action-oriented change that is fundamental to Tikkun Olam and the restoration of our broken world.

May we all repent one day before we die.

Paul Swehla

Book One

Creation

Prologue

Vessels

The King forms and fires earthen ware pots
He manipulates the vessels from the fire's angry embers
Hot water would crack them apart
Ice water, shrinking, contracting, will shatter to shards
"I'll mix them!" cries the King, and the vessels endure
Had G-d made His universe with only mercy
Sin would abound and flood the sea
Had G-d made a world with only what's just
This Olam Hazeh could no longer be
"Alas!" wept the Holy One, Blessed be He
Attribute of Justice mixed with Mercy
The King creates with elements pure
Blended this way, adam shall endure

Gilgul: Transmigration

ALEPH

The Ballad of Peer Gynt

He hails from Gudbrandstahl
Asbjornsen portrayed him to one and all
Ibsen to the stage, lingua universal
Grieg through music incidental

Great folks are known by the steeds they ride
Horse or pig or reindeer in the sky
Jack of all trades, master of none
Petrus Gyntus shall never die

O'er yonder lies Haegstadt
There, the fence, the turning point
Make a decision, take a drink
Embrace your fate by failing to think

Button Moulder, Button Moulder, recast your soul
His casting ladle is ready to go
Transmigrate, O collective soul
Come once again to repair our world

His name is Peer Gynt, he's reincarnate
Existential philosopher
Negligent soulmate
Button Moulder, casting ladle, this is fate

In the forest there is no guide
The Boyg, from beyond, you cannot hide
Poor little Solveig waiting with her wings
O, Gyntian Self, you've struck once again

Peer Gynt, megalomaniac
Obsessive-compulsive panic attack
Neurotic to the core, anti-social
Hipster riffraff, pick up your slack

O, wise one, and prophet, Emperor Gynt
Grant a soul to Anitra, the Queen
Dybbuks, demons and demented dreams
Your fabric is weak, tearing the seams

The Button Moulder will melt you down
Poetic justice will come to town
A little Peer Gynt in each of us
Yet mercy can still be found

Gilgul: Transmigration

BEIT

My Name is Peer Gynt

My name is Peer Gynt
I like to kill trolls
My father is Jon
Mother Aase, a Jew
A tangled web, who knew?
Lend me your ears
I will explain
Legend I am
More than two hundred years
Since my parents conceived
But ahead of myself
I get, you see
Today, I have a different name
Irrelevant
It's all the same
Different parents
I have as well
All of them
I honor all

But these matters are trivial
In the grand scheme of things
To miss the forest for the trees
Cliche, cliche
In any event
I am Peer Gynt
Reincarnate

GIMEL

Tikkun Olam

I will tell you a story
A secret word to the wise
Life review in the House of Judgment
Soul stands before the Beit Din
Adhere to the mitzvah, do a good deed
Obey the commandments and plant a new seed
Reparation of our broken world
Reincarnate if need be
Restore the world—Tikkun Olam
Play your part and set us free
This is the goal at which Torah aims
Elevate sparks from the shells in the dark
Or return to the earth plane
Again and again and again

Gilgul: Transmigration

DALET

Prelude to the Soul

Look to the earth where you plant your seed
Watch it sprout from the earth, you'll see
Some like it hot and some like it cold
Not he who plants nor he who sows
Can make the seedling grow

Beauty is held in the eye, you know
Balance is set by the scale just so
Wisdom and knowledge, it's plain to see
Justice at par with Mercy
To make the seedling grow

Your truth is relative
But truth by the way
One day we'll know what's going on
Revealed to all one day

There is a crown worn by a king
Man with his wife and Eternal Queen
Wings of a dove, let the Spirit flow
Tree of Life with roots below
Make the seedling grow

She gently moves from soul to soul
From where she comes we do not know
Life she gives, the Spirit—flow
With five levels of the soul
We as seedlings grow

HEI

Adam Kadmon & the Roots of the Soul

Prime configuration
Divine light
Primeval space
Single beam of light
Eyes, mouth, ears and nose
Light of the Infinite
Bursting forth
Creating Ten Sephirot

Light of the World, Adam Kadmon
Ein Soph, Infinite One
All souls sprout from primordial son
Each branch connects to the root of the soul

Sparks, sparks, everywhere bright
Bound to shells and husks of the night
Vessels forming to contain the light
Shattering, bursting, as if in spite

Holy light, uncontained
Escape the vessels, maimed
Nitzotzot—shattering sparks
Lower, darker realms
Fallen, fallen, sparks have fallen
Waiting to be restored
Elevate consciousness
Material world
Lift me!
Raise me!
Hark!
I am a spark!

VAV

Spilled Seed

Adam was a chronic masturbator
One hundred and thirty years
Masturbation kills
Souls in Adam's semen
Bastardized sons
Instant of ejaculation
Lonely souls with expectation
To enter the womb of Eve
But Adam chose to spill his seed
Lilith's ground, Night Scene
Lost, these souls wait to be born
Dark thoughts leech
When bodies conceive
Inherent part
I am one of these

How this is so
This is a result
Cain kills Abel in a bout
Talmud, Midrash and Zohar teach
Adam and Eve reject intercourse

Futile attempt to prevent bloodshed
Century, score and decade be
Lamech kills Cain
Don't misconceive
Abel's ability
O, how the sages sing!
Soul progeny
Root of Abel
Root of Cain

Soul roots doctrinaire
Adam Kadmon
Souls of Abel do descend
Reroute destiny
Birthing eventually
Seth's pedigree
But I am not
One of these

ZAYIN

Gilgul

Generations come and generations go
The earth remains forever
Incarnations come and incarnations go . . .
Master of the Universe
Mysterious and clever

Gilgul, gilgul
Come back again
Divine sparks fall so far
Elevate the soul
Feed the poor
Sheltered storm
Restore our broken world
Teshuva
Repentance
Tikkun Olam
Back-hand to the face
Turn your cheek in grace
Mashiach will come one day
To reconstruct The Place

*   *   *

Building in Babel
To end human pain
But not as a rebel of G-d, per se
We grope for peace in the heavenly realms
Speaking in tongues, we decreate
Bludgeoning brothers annihilate

Born again
Petrified heart
Drowned in the time of the flood
Egyptian slave
Baptism renewed
Nile conjured to blood
Another birth
Bricks without straw
For my role as a builder
Babel's fall
Working in blood
Fingers and bone
Building for Pharaoh
Crushed by a stone

At Sinai, receive Torah
Sanctify barren seed
Cross pollination quarantine
G-d offers Torah to the rest of the world
But her body rejects the remedy

Adam Kadmon, root of the soul
Two hundred forty-eight bones

Solar year of sinews
Living laws and codes
Six hundred thirteen mitzvot
Deed to body and soul

Ha Shem says "I am"
Betrothing Yisra'el
Na'aseh v'nishmah
We hear and obey

Sh'ma Yisra'el
Adonai Eloheinu
Adonai Echad

Hear, O Israel
The L-RD our G-d
The L-RD is One

But incarnations come
And incarnations go
The earth remains forever
A seed begins to grow

I kneel before the priest
On Israel's behalf

Golden earrings
Golden calf
Atoning crimson death

Life is in the blood
I'm hacked by the sword

I'm the goat for Azazel
In the wilderness
Time of Moshe's wrath
Shards of scripted stones
On that fateful day
Aaron points his finger
First of three mil slain
No land
No milk
No honey
But this, I need not say

Gilgul, gilgul
Incarnations come
And incarnations go
This sterile seed must germinate
On a different day

*   *   *

Divine insurrection
Refusal to repent

Gilgul: Transmigration

I am a darkened dybbuk
Disembodied soul

Roaming desert regions
Searching for weak souls
Mesopotamia
Bodies to possess

Compelling mortal vessels
Propelling evil deeds
Dwelling in my host
'Til exorcism death

Imprisonment
Lower astral plane
Earthbound spirit
Dead man I used to be

Two thousand years
Defying Adonai
Open revolt
Contra Beit Din

Free will decision
Gehenna certainly
Purify the soul
Purgatory

Not to Gan-Eden
But rein-carnation

Hell on earth again
Pain and suffering

Evil becomes still
Opening a door
Teshuva for a dybbuk
Not impossible

Evil turns to peace
Planting of a seed
Master of the Universe
Blessed be He

Soft'ning of the heart
Touch of Her hand
Dove is released
In search of dry land

Body's broken bones
Teshuva, action, choice
Thunderous alarm
Peeling shofar

Almighty Voice
Heard once again
From darkness to light
Before the Beit Din

Gilgul: Transmigration

CHET

The Dark side of the Moon

The dark side of the moon refuses to shine
Turn your back on the sun
The dark side of the moon can still be seen
Reflecting light as one

The light of the sun reflects off the earth
The dark side is seen
Even in the darkest place
Light is able to shine

Shofar, shofar, blowing at dusk
Light of the moon first seen
Shadowed whole and crescent moon
Begin the month of Elul

Call to repent, strike a chord
Deep within your soul
Caught off guard by this primal sound
Turning is good for the soul

Pyres erupt on the mountain top
Fires on mountains do flare
Teshuva and the call to repent
New moon, new month, new year

Shofar invokes fear and awe
Trembling soul to the core
Dark side of the moon, let go of the night
Return to the path of the light

Quivering, crying, quaking horn
Tekia, shevarim, truwah
Blasting shofar, ring out every morn
Entire month of Elul

Yom Truwah—Rosh Hashana
Creation of the world
Crescent moon, New Year's day
Begin the month of Tishrei

TET

Yamim Nora'im

I take possession of a black mangy dog
Presuming lesser evil
A fool toying with a triple beam
For dogs, too, do testify
Attentive before the Beit Din
For crimes against eternity

Inclined toward the home of a great Tzaddik
A righteous and holy saint
He extracts hidden sparks
From broken shards in the dark
Nitzotzot from klippot
At the door I bark
Rebbe speaks to me
The judge grants a plea
Canine soliloquy

*   *   *

I do not know the prayers
I do not know the words

To free my soul from bondage
From this wretched, painful world

Master of the Universe
Letters-Numbers heard
Aleph-Tav, A to Z
Arrange them into words

Aleph-Beit
Shin-Tav

Gimel-Dalet   Hei-Vav
Kuph-Resh   Pei-Tzaddi

Zayin-Chet
Samech-Ayin

Tet-Yod   Kaph-Lamed
Mem-Nun   Kaph-Lamed

Mem-Nun
Tet-Yod

Samech-Ayin   Peh-Tzaddi
Zayin-Chet   Hei-Vav

Kuph-Resh
Gimel-Dalet

Shin-Tav
Aleph-Beit

Blessed be Your Holy Name
Let my prayer be heard

         *   *   *

Rosh Hashana
Yom Kippur
Ten days intercede

Rebbe guides
Through space and time
Paths of wisdom seen

Consciousness
Enlightenment
Running of the heart

Permutation
Aleph-Beit
Journey of return

Dancing soul
Tree of Life
Adam Kadmon

Thirty-two paths of wisdom
Twenty-two letters seen
Ten digit permutation
Hebrew Aleph-Beit

One to Ten—Sephirot
Stand before Beit Din

Thirty-two paths of wisdom
G-d creates in three
Sephar, Sapar, Sippur
Text, Number, Word

Permutate twenty-two
Ten digits seen
Third, fourth, fifth dimension
Hypercubic sephirot
Redemption thus achieved

*   *   *

Twinkling of an eye
Tekia Gedolah
Last great blast
Of a giant shofar
Caught up in the clouds
Unify the Name

Wick of a candle
Burning in the night
Blue fire surrounds me
Awash in yellow flame

Emotive plea
Shake with fear
Barely visible

Ghostly
Wraithlike
Lips begin to vibrate

Sh'ma Yisra'el
Adonai Eloheinu
Adonai Echad

The L-RD is One
Unify the Name
Light of the Divine

Radiation
Bound as One
With Adam Kadmon

*   *   *

Double vulcan hands
Lifted to the eyes
Ears, nose and mouth
Rebbe blesses me
Peer within the lines:
Bless you and keep you

May Adonai
Shine His face upon you
And shower you with grace
Elevate Countenance
Bequest you with His peace

*　　*　　*

I stand before a three judge panel
Heavenly Beit Din

Punishment fits the crime
Severe it is indeed
Sentenced to Gehenna
For one entire day
Purging of the soul
For one thousand years
Ten hundred years
Millennial transmigrant
Not as Homo sapien
But rooted as a plant

A grain of wheat
I'd germinate
Thus spake Beit Din
My soul could not redeem
Until a mitzvah
Be performed
Vicariously

YOD

The Grain of Wheat

Time passes, darkened dybbuk, disembodied soul
Thousand year internment in Gehenna I am told
Beit Din declares my fate, reincarnate grain of wheat
Fully conscious, reminiscent, how the lives unfold
Sin and pain, suffering, recalling every element
Adam's seed, spilled on earth, Noah's message sent

Babel's tower, slave in Egypt, refusing to repent
Golden calf, remembering all experience
Searching deep within my soul, teshuva becomes possible
Histavut, serenity, soul will elevate
Breath of life, soul will grow, from its natural state
Gratitude, humility, love to meditate

Reincarnate, reoccurring pain and suffering
Terra infernus, repeatedly, with opportunity
Repair the world, Tikkun Olam, balance is the key
Histavut, equanimity, spiritual maturity
To enter into Gan Eden, first return to earth again
Come again, to germinate, but not as Homo sapien

Rocks, plants, animals—histavut—great work to do
Insults, accolades, immunity to germs
Cheshek—passion—love for G-d, willing to repent
Countering inclination Yetzer Hara
Elevate and purify, nitzotzot from klippot
Mind, body, soul—Yetzer Ha Tov—inclining
    toward the good

KAPH

The Seedling

The gavel strikes with thunder as I stand before Beit Din
Purgation in Gehenna, but not humanity
Watching as a farmer in the earth he plants his seed
Searching for the germ that my soul will one day seize
Realizing not this seed, but rather its offspring
A grain of wheat, yet to be formed, becomes my destiny

Dread and awe, trepidation, I begin to plead
Watching as the farmer moves on to plant the seed
The one to yield the grain, the one to bear my soul
Master of the Universe, Blessed be He
Discharge the debt, wash away, water which to germinate
Too much rain—heaven forbid!—will wash my seed away

Praying for this seed, and praying fervently
To germinate, procreate, eventually transmigrate
Sun and moon, roots emerge, following a storm
Embryonic energy, light bursting from its shell
Za Zen, humus rich, becoming earth and rain
Breath of life, Word of G-d, leaves begin to form

Abyss of fear, deep within, murder crows appear
Unfolding on the earth, devouring what grows
Snatching seedlings, no remorse, destroying
    what's been sown
"Not kosher, these crows!" I cry, "black birds,
    O G-d, please no!"
A duck or chicken, there's still a chance, but please
    not a crow!
The offsping of a kosher bird could still redeem my soul

The kashered bird, devoutly bled, healing cosmic energy
Birchat'mazon, recharging power, redemption of a soul
Perform a mitzvah, repair our world
The pious Jew who does these deeds
Will free my soul vicariously
But please, dear G-d, I humbly pray
    don't let it be a crow!

My plant begins to grow, producing a seed head
My soul attaches to a seed, would I be baked in bread?
A Jew might recite Hamotzi, the special blessing said
Be still my soul, purge the dread
The birds are gone, the husk is shed
My seed matures waiting to be harvested

*   *   *

Master of the good name appears to me
Young man at the age of thirteen

Soul is pure, he sits next to me
Righteous seeker of fallen sparks
Guiding countless flames
Eternal fire redemption

Engraving lessons taught by esoteric fathers
Baal Shem Tov capturing attention
Thirty-two letters in a circle placed
Wall going 'round two hundred thirty-one gates
Back and forth the circle oscillates
Pinnacle peace, high ecstasy
Evil abyss, lowest disease

Circle drawn upon the ground, Hebrew Aleph-Beit
Channel chronologically, systematically
Permutation, transformation, patterned formulation
Letters form, taking shape, in the physical
Mandala-gram, open gates, paths to meditate
Monolithic pillars—Stone Henge of ancient script
Protoplasmic elements, primordial creation
Five dimensions, space and time, cosmic transmigration
231 lines, twenty-two letters connect
Open doors, quantum leap, simulspacious being
Baal Shem engraving vision, telekenetic energy
Mind is clear, centered, circle, dome and sphere

*   *   *

Baal Shem, Baal Shem, creating a man
Israel waves his ancient mythic hand

Emerging from the dust, the crown, the clay, the head
Eyes, ears, nose and mouth, spectral lines are spread
Two hands emerge, pulling at the earth
Lifting body, Asiyah, no breath of life comes
       with this birth
Golem, golem, adjust the scale, equilibrium

Restoration, Tikkun Olam, Mashiach, World to Come
A child's game, G-d's hand shall not be forced
Incantation, mantra, meticulous reverse
Chanting Hebrew opposite, immaculate unbirth
Golem's hands and shoulders recede back to the earth
Lights extinguish in his eyes, nose, ears and mouth
Crown of the head begins to fade
Back to ash and dust from which it came

LAMED

Fear and Trembling

Fear and trembling, salvation's work
Body reduces to element
Distilled spirit, essential state
Purify and concentrate
Master of the Universe, blessed be He
Molecules, wheat seed
Distilled liqueur, spirits plead

Stored in a cask for ten long years
Waiting, wondering, pondering, praying
Meditating day and night
Heart begins to run
Return to the place
Kingdom, Foundation, my roots I embrace

The day finally comes to be harvested
Bound and threshed, strong men break my back
Loaded onto a cart in a burlap sack
Locked in a warehouse and stored on a rack

Alone and afraid, I go not to the mill
Where I'd hoped to be ground and baked into bread

To the distillery I'm shipped instead
Fermenting and changing, filled with dread

With fear and trembling I watch
My body reduced to element
Beneath me a fire is lit
Sublimating spirit

Purification in reverse
Master of the Universe, blessed be He
Transfiguring me, a tiny wheat seed
Blessing from a curse

Stored in a cask for ten long years
I pray to be blessed and consumed
At Simchat Torah with joyous dancing
Vicarious blessing via pious Jews

Gilgul: Transmigration

MEM

Poured Out, Bottled Up

Poured out, bottled up
Shipped to a traveler's inn
On a shelf, emptied out
Would I be redeemed?
Cosmic order, proper blessing
Torah observant Jew
Or drunken peasant, going home
To beat his helpless wife?
Suffering agony
Faithless ambiguity
Tired and weary traveler
Entering the inn
    Torah-keeping Jew
    Kippa and the fringe

Waiting, watching, hopes are high
I see my prayers sail in the sky
Molecular body poured out at last
Peddler raises his drinking glass
Dreadful horror! Tragic shame!
Trifler fails to invoke the Name
Baruch Shem—bless the Name

Baruch atah Adonai
B'rocha—cosmic blessing
So weary, tired and dry
Neglecting this urgent deed
He fails to play his part
    Tikkun Olam, repair our world
    Miscarriage of a soul

NUN

Son of Jon and Aase Gynt

Begin anew, another breath
Incarnations come and go . . .
Ten more years, awaiting hope
Vicariously atone
Redeem the charge, incarnation
Cosmic restoration
Power blessing, b'rocha
Enough to free a soul
Reborn to a Nordic Drunk
Apostate Jewish wife
Egg, sperm and embryo
Jon and Aase Gynt
    Transmigration of the soul
    Hello, my name's Peer Gynt

Gilgul: Transmigration

SAMECH

Mother Aase

Mother Aase nurtures me with binding devil's yarn
She smothers me, we cling in desperate need
Mother Aase ever laments, O the wailing cries
Terrible agony, to look fate in the eyes

Father Gynt abandons us, we fend for ourselves
Forsaken land of ice and snow, forgotten in the cold
Sorrowful, sensual, intimate flesh
O, the many games we play in order to keep warm

    Burn many bridges, break many things
    Better not to give, but rather receive
    Exiled, I am, banned to the woods
    Flee to the Halls of the Mountain King

Eloping princess, usurping right, Jocosta
    Queen of Thebes
Intensely familiar dysfunctional sex, I am Oedipus Rex!
Liqueur and lies, fairy tale nectar sucked dry
Ambrosial bride rape in the night
    opiatic reindeer in the sky

Gnomes, trolls, pixies, sprites
Wipe the slate clean, magic might
Devil's yarns weaved in my head
Resurrect the Boyg from the dead

I am both troll and man
Ode to my Gyntian Self!
To myself I am enough!
I am father Gynt!

AYIN

The Ballad of Aase Gynt

I, Mother Aase, was a pious saint
Praying, obeying G-tt
One day came when I fell faint
Setting aside mitzvot

Planning Pesach, beginning to fret
Anticipating guests
"I must take the time," I said to myself
"To observe the minor mitzvot"

Another Voice spoke to me
The guests would soon arrive
"Not enough time," said the Yetzer Hara
The Voice from the Other Side

"It won't make a difference," said the Voice from Beyond
"To skip one prayer, one time
You are good, you love G-d
The Master knows your heart"

G-tt would forgive my failing of part
I agreed that G-tt would forgive
But another Voice began to prod
A Voice inclining toward good

The Yetzer Ha Tov spoke to me
"Repent and pray to redeem"
My sin weighed heavy upon my heart
Deliberate sin frightened me

Time passed, I did not pray
I was not struck dead that day
My guests arrived, we wept for joy
It was a beautiful day

The Button Moulder showed my son
This beginning of my end
My sin alone, he went on to tell
Would not condemn me to Hell

But Satan himself pressed charges in court
He snatched a hold of the sin
Up to Heaven he went with his claim
And argued before the Beit Din

All three judges of the Beit Din
Would not convict for one sin
But Satan knew best of all
Sin begets more sin

Each sin lowers the world
Deeper into the dark
Each good deed repairs the world
Elevate the spark

Olam Hazeh, this broken world
Lucifer as king protects
Jamming traffic of Tikkun Olam
To prolong the coming of the L-rd

Bound by spells and incantations
Deeper into sin
Myths and legends, pagan nations
Embracing I did begin

Coitus sacra, Norse deities
Sacrilegious tart
I slipped deeper into sin
With hatred toward my kin

I secretly planned my escape
I would seal my fate
To run away, assimilate
On a future date

Before I could unveil my scheme
My life became a dream
Karma wears a yarmulke
Of darkened energy

The Jews from my community
Were falsely accused
"For killing a child and draining his blood
For use in unleavened bread"

Blood libel, twenty-four Jews
Indicted during Lent
Twelve martyred, twelve "repent"
O, how the soul is rent!

Mother marrano, fleeing I went
My husband, Jon Gynt
Button Moulder disappears
Leaving me Peer Gynt

Casting ladle in his hand
He seems to have no fear
Pathetic gift from his father dear
A Button does appear

Moulding buttons, dictate fate
Transmigrate
Silver button without defect
The loop will never break

Good Christian Peerkin Gynt
Son of Jon Gynt
You're not a Jew! You're not a Jew!
Christians murder you!

Gilgul: Transmigration

I'll protect you from the fright
With gnomes, trolls and sprites
I'm your queen, and you're my king
We'll kill the Trolls of Night

Gilgul: Transmigration

PEH

The Boyg

Engulfed in darkness, pitch black, I stand
Here in the presence of the invisible Boyg
Monstrous troll of Nordic lore
Devoid of purpose, filled with dread
Confronted by me, a still small voice
Charred wood, burnt forest
I prepare to fight the Boyg 'til death

What are you?
Who are you?
Fight, you fool!

But the Boyg refuses
I do not yield

Teshuva calls upon great strokes
Borne upon wings of a giant dove
Contrition, penitence, a turning point
Wafted by wings, this holy, sacred love
She beckons me, gently prodding
I harden my heart, turn my back and refuse

Ring the church bells
Hymns to the rescue
The women will save

Not to myself am I true
To myself I am enough, troll, thru and thru

Gilgul: Transmigration

TZADDI

Night Scene

Thread balls and withered leaves
Sighing in the air
Bear witness against me

Souls confined, trapped for a time
Solveig, my queen, I've abandoned thee
Gyntian self subdued at Beit Din

Souls of Adam before the flood
Dreading repentance, rejecting the blood
Dark angels testify when I die

The past haunts like a woman in green
The soul is bound to the deed
Mother in the cold until she's freed

Button Moulder does not damn me to Hell
Though I'm banished, I forgive their lot
They slay me but I falter not

I bear this lonesome burden
I must, I do, I will
I'm their scapegoat, christened Azazel

This is Night, the Night Scene

KUPH

Dark Angels

I learn of Mother's plight
Dark angels testify in the night
Against me
The Night Scene
Idea of repentance
Fills me with dread
Treadballs
Withered leaves
Sighing in the air
Dewdrops
Broken dreams
Thoughts I should have thought
Words unspoken
Deeds undone
Freedom to choose
Fail to respond
Relinquish freedom
Terror
Responsibility

I, like Onan, spill my seed
My own dark angels
Testify
Against me

Mother Aase cries out from the ice and snow
Lamenting her loss of liberty
Accountability
Solveig, my soulmate, mitzvah denied
Forfeit redemption
By and by
Paid in full
Gilgul

RESH

Lilith

Lilith comes to me in my dreams
Disguised as both and all of you
Lilith comes to me at night
Coming twice for each of you

Seducing with erotic stealth
Deprive the soul of all its wealth
Leaving nothing but an empty shell
Dreams of pleasure, visions of Hell

*   *   *

Mother's soul, interred as a dybbuk
Soria-Moria, north of the castle
Upon the glacial shelf
Much of her life
Bound to Lilith's djinn
Refusing to repent
For our conjugal sin
We choose not to part

With the comfort of our shame
Solveig, my queen
I abandon thee
And hereby reroute destiny

SHIN

The Master & the Mouse

"You are not worthy of Hell!"
This is what the Button Moulder yelled

The Rebbe taught his talmudim
Conjuring memories
Betrayal in a time gone by
Cause of immense suffering

The Master set a trap
A rodent caught, unharmed
"You will not escape judgment
Merely through Death's arm"

Pleading with the Rebbe
I beg to change my fate
Terminate my suffering
No longer reincarnate

"But do not simply kill me
To transmigrate spectrum wide
Please, instead, send me to Hell
Where my soul will purify"

The Master's mandate to my mouse:
"Throughout this world you'll roam
Repent one day before you die
You're not worthy of Gehinnom!"

Opening the Mouse's trap
The Master sets me free
Returning to the suffering
Of reincarnate me

TAV

Soulmates

You and I, we are soulmates
We're destined to find each other
But it doesn't always work out this way
Free will choice can abort destiny

Each soul, egress, Adam Kadmon
Intertwined with its opposite
Male and female come as one
Preconceived androgeny

Lower realms divide the soul
Reunite, Solveig, Night Scene
A troll 'til the end, myself enough
Content to do as I please

Every soul's light transcends
Two becoming one above
Bearing light, welkin bound
Two lights merge as one

False soulmates, phantoms distract
Angels decree destiny
Arousal, attachment, desires attract
False soulmates seduce, I'll have to come back

Epilogue

The Goat Thief

Starving, I steal a goat: I kill it, I clean it, I cook it
I feed it to my wife and kids

Found guilty, my penalty, five years
    of indentured servitude
And five silver coins, a debt I cannot pay

The auction begins, humbled I stand
    before my community
First call, chief brick layer, five years and five silver coins

A piercing cry stabs my ear by a doctor of the law
Four years of labor and six silver coins
    my service he tries to retain

Yet to be sold, the baker bellows a bargaining bid
Three years of baking bread, seven shekels of silver
    I crumble before my peers

We're finally sold, my family and I, to the Master carpenter
Eight silver coins, the gavel is struck
    two years of servitude

Five silver coins for the heir of the goat
    three to community chest
For teaching a trade, instructing a way for the widows,
    orphans and poor

Yara Torah—Word of G-d—the way, the truth, the life
Beyond the law, to teach and instruct
    my kids, myself, my wife

The chief carpenter is a pious saint
The law is tempered by grace

Book Two

Revelation

Lightning Flashes

Lightning flashes from heaven to earth
    Three pillars stand
    Seven levels ascend

Atomic bombs of energy transcend our world
    Radiant three hover above
        Emanation
        Creation
        Formation
    Living, breathing babies
        Action
    Reborn

Gilgul: Transmigration

Avot: Visions of the Fathers

Prelude to the Fathers

I stand at the foot of the mount
Thick clouds roil and stew in a great caldron
Thunder, lightning and the blast of a shofar
Six hundred thousand souls stand wraithlike
Trembling with fear and awe before El Shaddai

Smoke envelops the mountain
Fire descends and the earth quakes
A Voice booms from the heavens
Teaching, instructing
Commanding mitzvot

We respond as one: "Na'aseh v'nishmah"
We hear, do and obey Ha Shem

Kol Yisra'el yesh lachem chelek la olam
All Israel has a share in the world to come

Gilgul: Transmigration

Perek Rishon—Vision One

The fathers and elders
Prophets, Priests and Kings
Say to their children, grow many things
The land shall be yours
The world changes with action
Justice, Mercy and Peace

Cover yourselves with the dust of wise feet
Kick dust from your feet at fools, but be discreet
Say little and do much
The world is preserved in this way
Choose wisely and give what you receive
With Truth: Justice, Mercy and Peace

Gilgul: Transmigration

Perek Sheni—Vision Two

A painting by Dali with landscape surreal
An eyeball hovers in the sky
Watching all deeds
An ear floats nearby
Hearing all that we say

Dancing quill in hand
With book below
Deeds transcend
A Voice then booms:
"Trust not thyself 'til death!"

Judge not lest ye be judged
Lead when there are no wise men to follow
A distant river flows
On the surface floats a skull
It's all very clear to me

The karmic rule applies
To drown means to drown
What comes around goes around
A Voice then booms:
"So repent one day before you die!"

Gilgul: Transmigration

Perek Shelishi—Vision Three

A man appears at my side
Not a soul, per se, but flesh and blood
Etching words upon my stone
The granite of my soul

He tells me all I need to know
In order to keep from falling short
To no longer miss the mark
From where I've come
To where I'll go
I'll one day have my day in court

You come from the putrefying drop
You'll go to dust, worm and maggot
To account for action, taken and not
Before the King of kings, blessed be He
Everything is foreseen
But freedom of choice is given

Gilgul: Transmigration

Perek Revi'i—Vision Four

The world is an ante-chamber
To the Olam Haba
Prepare yourself in the waiting room
That you may enter the hall

I see a bottle of wine
He tells me to look rather to the wine inside
He points to a little man, green from jealousy
    lustful ambition
A shepherd drives him like a sheep from a place unwanted

Gilgul: Transmigration

Perek Chamishi—Vision Five: The Ten Sayings

A brilliant panorama unfolds before my eyes
Light, color, wind, water, fire and air
Geometric shapes, raw earth
Tohu v'bohu—chaos and void
Lines marking dimensions, foundation is set
Cornerstone laid

The morning stars begin to sing
The sea is restrained by enormous blockades
Huge gates!
Her womanhood is concealed in darkness
    and thick clouds
Green growth and foliage
Marvelous creatures!

The Ten Sayings begin to take form
Emanating
Being from the backdrop of chaos and void
I see what is both tree and man
Revealed, I understand
This is the embodiment of life

I see Adam Kadmon
Sephirot—Numbers, letters
Building blocks of creation
Etz Chayim hi!
She is a tree of life
Creation!

ALEPH—With Wisdom, "Let there be light"

BEIT—With Understanding, "Let there be a firmament"

GIMEL—With Love, "Let the waters be gathered"

DALET—With Strength, "Let the earth put for grass"

HEI—With Beauty, "Let there be luminaries
    in the firmament"

VAV—With Victory, "Let the waters swarm
    with living creatures"

ZAYIN—With Splendor, "Let the earth bring
    forth living creatures"

CHET—With Foundation, "Let us make man
    in our image"

TET—With Kingship, "Behold, I give you every herb"

YOD—Crowned with Kingship
    "The beginning is embedded in the end"

The Yod is the Ten Sayings

From beginning to end

From Aleph to Tav

The Word is made flesh

From Tav to Aleph

Tabernacling among us

The end is embedded in the beginning

Word existing in Yod

Perek Shishi—Vision Six

I turn to look
Elijah—ergo—the Button Moulder
Is nowhere to be found
A Voice from beyond:
Yara Emet—Torah of Truth
Which include all worlds
Bereshit bara Elohim
Et hashamayim v'et ha aretz
In the beginning G-d creates
The heavens and the earth
Sh'ma Yisra'el
Adonai Eloheinu
Adonai Echad
Hear, O Israel
The L-RD our G-d
The L-RD is One
The Button Moulder appears at my side
Singing the chorus of the song

Gilgul: Transmigration

Coda: Awakening

The Button Moulder disappears and I wake
 from my dream
These visions reoccur through life, flowing in a stream
These ethics have been etched upon the granite
 of my soul
Still, I refuse to repent, I cannot redeem

Each time I awake, a Second-Self observes my Self
From beyond, another time, place and realm
The Other, No. 2 observing No. 1 at the helm
The Other prods for teshuva as One does refuse

Awakening each time to church bells, hymns and psalms
The Boyg, from beyond, thunders aloud
"Go 'round about, Peer Gynt!
Stop, turn and go 'round about!"

Gilgul: Transmigration

Shabbat

Visions of Mother
Tabla Sacra
Esoteric erotica
Braided loaf of bread
Candles
Wine
Hands before her head
Wafting
Sacred Words
Silent, sung and said
Hebrew blessings
Drinking wine
Ecstasy
Eating bread
Family
Friends
Things I'd never seen
The Sabbath bride is wed

Gilgul: Transmigration

Kavannah

Heartfelt movement
Clearing of the fog at dawn
Solar warmth filling your home
Eucalyptus, chamomile and camphor
Empty the mind
The Spirit moves
Shalom: Zen, flow, peace, gel, om

Gilgul: Transmigration

Shalom Alecheim

The Button Moulder reveals a vision of my life unlived
The sun sets as I walk along an empty street
Agents appear from beyond
One shines with light
The other walks in the shade
On either side they accompany me
From shul to Shabbat's sanctity

The Old Man knows how the story ends
Stars and planets align
Time pieces
Determinism
Voluntary will
At peace with paradox
I seek blessing from these kings
"Shalom alecheim," I sing
Alecheim shalom
"Peace unto you"

Peace unto you
Minist'ring kings
Angels of the Most High
Blessed be He

Peace unto you
May you come in peace
Bless me for peace
May you depart in peace

Candles lighted upon linen cloth
Fine china adorns all around
My wife and children, I embrace
By order of our will
Messenger of light acquires the right
Sustaining the right to speak first
May it be so in the coming week
May Shabbat be sanctified
By the order of His will, the dark angel speaks
Compelled, he says, "Amen"

All coins have two sides as men have two hands
I enter my home and there's no one inside
My wife and I have divided our pride
Gone with the children, I'm left all alone
The messenger of night acquires the right
Sustaining the right to speak first

Gilgul: Transmigration

May it be so in the coming week
Shabbat be defiled and profaned
By the cosmic order of His ways
The angel of light says, "Amen"

*   *   *

Bless the children, the power is cosmic
Channel energy, healing tonic
Effect is immediate, pebble in a pond
Commutation of a thousand souls
Enter free will and humility
Wife, children and family
Alter order of infinite beings
Mitzvot and good deeds
As father, priest and king
I bless my family

Universal blessing
World to Come
Damage in need of repair
Shalom alecheim
When all is restored
Mashiach will come
Tikkun Olam

Book Three

Redemption

Gilgul: Transmigration

Yiddische Neshamah

I am born as a Lithuanian Gentile from an aristocratic family. At Oxford, I study the doctrines of Christianity. I am exposed to the major religions of the world as I prepare for ordination. I become enamored by the truth, majesty and beauty I discover in Judaism and, like a lover with his beloved, I approach her as if she were a mare harnessed to one of Pharaoh's chariots.

I understand Jesus as a Jew. His Hebrew name, Yeshua, means that salvation comes in the name of Yah. A tender shoot, a root from dry ground, G-d smites this ugly, leper-loving fellow. The epitome of suffering, he is despised and rejected by mankind, and he carries AIDS and Ebola upon his shoulders. He is a servant who does nothing but suffer. He has not come to this earth to start a new religion, nor is he the Christ of Christianity; He is the Messiah of the Jews. Still, the Rabbis refuse.

Gangrenous is the wound of hatred that this man's wife harbors. She despises her Semitic mother and copulates fiercely with her pagan father. She is obsessed with phallic symbols, sun deities and ritualistic fertility. She's unable to smell the rotten stench of her own decay. A whore, she is oblivious to the contractual liabilities she assumes under the law that her husband clearly did not nail to the cross. "Grace! Mercy!" she cries as she fornicates with the wild olive tree of her ancestors. Her concept of vicarious atonement is acted out and justified by blood libel and pogroms. This is to say nothing of her blatant violation of Shabbat which, like her harlotry, is punishable by divorce and death. I am intimately aware of Jesus the Jew. Oh, the leavening in the bread! I am revolted and capitulate out of disgust.

I drop out of seminary in my final year. I wander throughout eastern Europe, often returning home to Eishyshok. I roam to the northeast and I am welcomed by a small Hasidic community in Lyady. I sit at the feet of the Lubavitcher Rebbe. It is here where I enter into covenant with the G-d of Avraham, Yitz'chak and Ya'akov. I am cut and immersed—blood and water flow. I deny Yeshua and convert to Judaism. I publicly renounce faith in Jesus and false deities: I deny Yeshua as Messiah, Savior and Redeemer of the world. Like an ox, I take on the yoke of a plow. I am blasphemer, apostate and heretic: I am plague.

My Jewish brothers marvel at my dexterity, my ability to shoot and make the mark. They believe that I have a Yiddische Neshamah, a Jewish soul. I am present at Sinai. I do not make it to Gan Eden because I am destined to reincarnate. I must perform a mitzvah I've failed to perform in past lives. I am a lost sheep that finds her way back to the fold. My spark is lifted. I am faithful to the bride of Torah. I am recognized as a tzaddik, a righteous one. Eventually, I am ordained as a rabbi.

Yet the shell feels empty while the nut remains.

One Less Death

And so I marry a good Jewish girl
Not my soulmate, Solveig

Unhappy with my marriage
I seek the Rebbe for advice
My wife's an insufferable hag
Nagging, complaining, day and night
Not knowing what else to do
A divorce would end our fight

The Rebbe fixes his eyes
Slipping into a trance
He bores deep within my soul
Reading my book of past lives
A time without end, he's conscious again
Pathos on his front, a deep sigh

The punishment for idolatry is death
This sin compounds an enormous debt
A thousand deaths cannot atone
But death's decree cannot be deemed
    by subastral Beit Din
The Beit Din of Gan Eden declares a different fate
For all the Jews who've fallen short

Rebbe goes on to explain
My backlogged list of death penalties
Carried over from past lives
Impossible it is to atone for my sins
There's simply not enough time
Before Mashiach arrives

In G-d's infinite mercy, I'm given my wife
Worse than a thousand deaths
When times come that I can stand her no more
I'm accounted with dying one more death
I say under my breath as she nags and complains
"Baruch ha Shem—Bless the Name—for one less death"

One day my wife hears what I say
I speak of my time with the Rebbe
In spite of my wife being a shrew
She's a pious hasid, an upright Jew
Respecting the Rebbe, resenting her role
She stops her kvetching, there's peace in our home

The Crucial Mitzvah

Before the Beit Din
Life review
Yiddische Neshamah
Good news, bad news

Jewish soul
Faithful to my wife
My soul atones
Death decrees
But one crucial mitzvah
I fail to obey
But it cannot be
Revealed by Beit Din
I must perform
Independently

Soul given three clues
For Mashiach's delay
A mitzvah failed
Collectively
Yiddische Neshamah
All Jewish souls
Culminate
Mitzvah commencing
Messianic Age

Mystical Torah
Summed in Grace
This reason alone
Gentiles have a place
In the Olam Haba
The World to Come

This crucial mitzvah
Says the Beit Din
Simpler to do
As a Goy
But not as a Jew

I'm born again
My parents are
Torah observant
Conceive on Shabbat
They name me Shalom
A Goy I am not

Shalom

I am a Torah scholar
Talmudist
Rabbi
Saint
Yet something hungers in my soul
I am incomplete

Master of Kabbalah
Esoteric thought
Elevating consciousness
Through prayer and mitzvot

Love to meditate
Upon the Ein Soph
The Infinite One
Crowns of Justice
Peace
And Mercy
Mystically triune

Three Steps exist within Themselves
Neither One nor apart from the Others
The Holy One, blessed be He
Revealed as One in Three Heads

One Head is exalted Three Times
Ein Soph
The Infinite One
As Three
As Two
As One
The Crown of all Perfection
The Feminine One

Tetragrammaton is revealed
Eliyahu ha Navi
TaNaKh in tandem with B'rit Hadasha
Torah
Neva'im
Ketuvah
Creation
Revelation
Redemption
Renewed Covenant
Yeshua ha Mashiach ben Yoseph
One day come again
Mashiach ben David
Return and reign as King

I publicly confess before my fold
Yeshau ha Mashiach
King of the World
Jews need not convert
Heaven forbid!
Remain as a Jew

Dance with Torah
Embracing Yeshua
As the man he claims to be

First time in my life
There's peace within my soul
Community is stunned
I forfeit my place
"The mystery of Torah is revealed through Grace!"
I'm forced to resign
I'm accompanied by
A third of my fold

Damned by the Elders
Branded apostate
Talmudic words dictate
To sin overtly is worse than murder
To mislead Jews from the faith
A trifle to rob flesh from this world
A tragedy it truly is
To remove a soul from the World to Come
Better to kill in Olam Hazeh
Than to rob from Olam Haba

I'm ridiculed
Ostracized
Banished like a fool
Cut off from my people
Exiled from the shul

My family disowns me
My father says Kaddish
A funeral's held on my behalf
Yet I remain at peace

Gilgul: Transmigration

Aliyah

I do Aliyah
Appeal to rabbinical powers that be
To vacate and remand
Conduct and prove
Yeshua's innocence
Truth of his mission
Exonerate his name
For all the world to see

Tikkun Olam
Jacob's children
Brother Joseph
Mashiach ben Yoseph
Yeshua's return
Messianic Age
Mashiach ben David
Kingdom of G-d
Olam Haba

He will return
Yerushalayim cries
"Baruch haba b'shem Adonai!"
Blessed be He
Who comes in the Name of the L-RD!

Glossary

Adam Kadmon: (1) Primordial man; (2) the Divine Light that flows from the Ein Soph (G-d) to all creation; (3) source and root of all souls; (4) the 613 commandments, or mitzvot, of Torah.

Adonai: L-rd. Lit., my L-rd. Adonai represents the feminine aspect of G-d. ADONAI is a sacred name of G-d; cf. Isa. 6:1.

Aleph-Beit: (1) The Hebrew alphabet; (2) the building blocks of creation.

Aliyah: To ascend or go up. On the temporal level, aliyah means to ascend or go up to the land of Isreal; to emmigrate to Israel. On a spiritual level, aliyah means to ascend to heaven, or Gan Eden.

Avot: Lit., fathers (sing., Av). Avot often refers to "Pirkei Avot," a fundamental text from the Mishna, primarily concerned with ethics, often translated: Ethics of the Fathers.

Azazel: A demon or evil spirit to whom the scapegoat was sent on Yom Kippur, the Day of Atonement; cf. Lev. 16.

Baal Shem Tov: Lit., Master of the good name. Israel ben Eliezer, b. 1700; d. 1760. Polish Jew and Rabbi; founder and first Rebbe of Hasidism.

Baruch atah Adonai: Blessed are you L-RD... A formula that begins many Hebrew blessings.

Baruch [ha] Shem: Bless the Name [of G-d] (cf. Halleluyah—Praise G-d).

Beit Din: Lit., House of Judgment. A rabbinical court of law. On earth, this three-judge panel decides civil cases. In heaven, spiritual matters are decided, usually resulting in one of three destinations for the soul: (1) reincarnation so as to further Tikkun Olam; (2) a stint in Gehenna for cleansing purification and reincarnation; or (3) to Gan Eden, or Paradise.

Birchat ha Mazon: Blessing and thanksgiving recited after meals praising the Creator of the Universe for sustenance and provision. Like all blessings and commandments, or mitzvot, "Birchat ha Mazon" is believed to have cosmic significance and consequence when either performed or neglected.

B'rit Hadasha: The New or Renewed Covenant. Hebraicized term to represent the New Testament.

B'rocha: (pl. B'rachot) Blessing or benediction. Blessings elevate spiritual consciousness and elevate Nitzotzot—Holy Sparks of Divine Light—that hasten Tikkun Olam and repair our broken world.

Cheshek: A powerful state of consciousness or spiritual enlightenment attained through prayer and meditation; where blessings and curses that come from the lower spiritual realms no longer influence the adept; a passionate yearning for the Divine; see Histavut.

Dybbuk: A dead person's disembodied soul, unable to attain peace because of sins unaccounted for in a past life. A dybbuk is a soul that has not been before the beit din for judgment, usually out of refusal or rebellion. Dybbuks often possess the living and can be exorcised.

Ein Soph: Lit., No End or Infinite Nothingness. The Infinite One, the Supreme Deity or G-dhead.

Elohim: Sacred name of G-d; attribute of Justice and Judgment; cf. Gen. 1:1.

El Shaddai: Sacred Name of G-d, meaning Mighty El or G-d; cf. Gen. 17:1.

Eliyahu ha Navi: Elijah the Prophet, often appearing in visions as a spiritual advisor or guide.

Gehenna: (Gehinnom) Often translated as purgatory, or loosely, hell; spiritual realm where souls are cleansed and purified; opposite of Gan Eden.

Gemara: Lit., Completion. Commentary on the Mishna; together with the Mishna, the Gemara "completes" the Talmud.

Gilgul: Hebrew term for the transmigration of souls meaning cycle or revolve; reincarnation. The purpose of gilgul is not only to perfect the soul through successive levels, but to repair the world. Tikkun Olam is accomplished in part through gilgul as the soul is elevated through the performance of mitzvot.

G-d/G-tt: Reverent designation for the Name of the Creator of the universe, blessed be He. Written in this manner to preserve the sanctity of the name; used to ensure that the Name is not used in vain, blasphemed nor destroyed. (G-tt designates the Germanic variation of this tradition.)

Golem: A created being that does not possess a G-dly soul, or Neshamah. The golem is created through perfect recitation and permutation of certain letters of the Hebrew aleph beit, especially those of the Tetrammaton, a sacred Name of G-d. A golem is a servant to its master and creator.

Goy: (1) A gentile or pagan; (2) Lit., Nation, or one from among the nations (pl. goyim) other than Israel.

Hamotzi: Blessing recited to the L-RD G-d, Master of the Universe for the provision of bread from the earth. Like all blessings, commandments, and mitzvot, Hamotzi has cosmic repercussions when performed or neglected.

HaShem: Lit., The Name used to prevent the profanation and desecration of the sacred Name of G-d, cf. Lev. 24:11.

Hasid/Hasidic/Hasidism: One who is pious and upright, Torah observant; affiliated with Hasidism, the mystical movement within Orthodox Judaism, founded by the Baal Shem Tov and dedicated to strict observance to commandments and mitzvot of Torah.

Histavut: A mystical state of equilibrium or equanimity; spiritual maturity attained by intense prayer and meditation (e.g., formulated recitation and permutation of the Hebrew aleph beit). At this spiritual level, the adept is able to completely dispel the Yetzer Hara, or evil inclination; see Cheshek.

Kabbalah: (1) Lit., Received doctrine or tradition; (2) esoteric, mystical, occult teachings used to interpret the Hebrew Scriptures; (3) Jewish theosophy, cosmology and philosophy.

Kaddish: Important mystical blessing recited upon a loved one's death, the anniversary of their death and also during daily Jewish prayer; related to kodesh, holy or sacred.

Kavannah: Intent, intention, both legally and morally; (1) spiritual devotion with intent to achieve devakut, a certain level of communion with G-d; (2) loosely, the movement of the Spirit behind the ritual.

Kippa: Hebrew term for yarmulke or skullcap.

Kosher/Kasher: Ritual purification and slaughter of food in accordance with the dietary laws of Torah; a mitzvah with cosmic significance.

Lilith: Adam's first wife, turned demon and sexual tyrant; created before Eve; night witch and vampire; she haunts deserted places and torments children and wayward souls.

Lubavitcher: Sect of Hasidic Judaism founded in and named after Lubavitch, a town in Russia. First Lubavitcher Rebbe: Schneur Zalman of Lyady.

Mashiach: Messiah; anointed one.

Mashiach ben David: Messiah—son of David—as reigning king of Israel and the world.

Mashiach ben Yoseph: Messiah—son of Joseph—as suffering servant and king of the world.

Midrash: (1) Lit., To search out the meaning of scripture beyond the literal interpretation; (2) application of story, parable, and legend as a tool for teaching, instruction, illumination and interpretation of Torah; (3) part of the Oral Torah and major source of early kabbalistic thought.

Mishna: Oral Torah committed to writing in the third century C.E. The Gemara (compiled in the fifth century C.E.) serves as a commentary to—or literally, the completion of—the Mishna; together, the Mishna and the Gemara constitute the Talmud.

Mitzvah: (pl. Mitzvot) Commandment, good deed, duty, obligation, responsibility, etc. (1) There are 613 mitzvot, or commandments, of the Torah, 248 positive and 365 prohibitive (representing, respectively, the bones and sinews of Adam Kadmon); (2) action such as teshuva or repentance; (3) examples of mitzvot include observing Shabbat, visiting the sick, avoiding evil speech, Torah study and charity, etc.; (4) Prerequisite for Tikkun Olam, i.e., steps in the redemption process; (5) broadly, active elevation of the soul; see B'rocha and Nitzotzot.

Na'aseh v'nishmah: We will hear and obey all that ADONAI has spoken; words spoken collectively by Israel while at Sinai, entering into covenant with YHVH.

Neshamah: one of the five levels of the human soul; also known as the G-dly soul.

Neva'im: Prophets; the second part of the Hebrew Scriptures in their traditional arrangement; see TaNaKh and Torah.

Nitzotzot: (1) Holy sparks, divine light brought into existence during creation; (2) mitzvot; (3) souls. Nitzotzot are bound and trapped within the husks and shells of evil (klipot) in this physical world and must be elevated and restored in order to achieve Tikkun Olam (e.g., through prayer, meditation, good deeds and other mitzvot). (This is not to confuse the human body as being innately evil in any way.)

Olam Haba: (1) The world to come; (2) the Messianic Age; (3) the Kingdom of Heaven.

Olam Hazeh: This present world, to end in a day of judgment and begin Olam Haba.

Pirkei Avot: Usually translated: Ethics of the Fathers. This ethical treatise is a major part of the Mishna.

Perek: (pl. pirkei) Chapter, ethic; loosely, vision.

Pesach: Passover, commemoration of the Exodus from Egypt; see Ex. 12.

Rebbe: Rabbi, teacher, and more precisely, enlightened spiritual guide and master; tzaddik.

Rosh Hashana: Lit., Head of the Year. (1) Jewish new year (civil) and anniversary of the creation of the world; (2) synonymous with Yom Truwah—the Day of Blowing [the Shofar].

Sapar: Text; Sefer Yetzirah 1:1.

Sephar: Number; Sefer Yetzirah 1:1.

Sippur: Word; Sefer Yetzirah 1:1.

Sephirot: (sing., sephirah) Lit., Numbers, Letters; (1) emanations from the Ein Soph or G-dhead; (2) archetypes of creation; (3) the Tree of Life.

Shabbat: Sabbath; seventh day of the week (from sundown on Friday to sundown on Saturday); sacred day of the covenant between YHVH and Israel.

Shalom Alecheim: (1) Traditional greeting meaning, Peace unto you. (2) Traditional song sung during the Shabbat ceremony with extremely kabbalistic overtones.

Sh'ma: Quintessential statement of faith and Jewish raison d'etre; cf. Dt. 6:4–9; 11:13–21; Num. 15:37–41 (Dt. 22:12).

Sh'ma Yisra'el Adonai Eloheinu Adonai Echad: "Hear O Israel, the L-RD our G-D, the L-RD is One." Dt. 6:4.

Shofar: Ram's horn used ritually and symbolically; blown on Rosh Hashana/Yom Truwah and Yom Kippur; the sound of the shofar, and the symbolism it represents, serves as a reminder of: (1) the Creator and His Kingship; (2) the call to do teshuva; (3) the Revelation at Mt. Sinai (Ex 19:19); (4) the voice of the Prophets; (5) the destruction of the Temple; (6) the binding of Isaac (Gen. 22; i.e., faith, trust, sacrifice, obedience, repentance); (7) imminent danger; (8) the day of judgment; (9) the redemption of Israel; and (10) the resurrection of the dead. The shofar is also symbolic of the coming of the Messiah and Olam Haba.

Shul: (1) Synagogue; (2) house of Torah study.

Simchat Torah: Lit., Joy of the Torah; Jewish holy day celebrating the end and new beginning of the yearly cycle of Torah readings; observers dance joyously in procession with the Torah scroll. Simchat Torah immediately follows the harvest festival of Sukkot.

Sukkot: Jewish harvest festival variously known as the Feast of the Ingathering, Tabernacles or Booths, celebrating the Creator's provision for the world and commemorating the time when YHVH provided for Israel while in the desert of Sinai.

Talmud: To learn; Jewish teaching and instruction comprised of the Mishna and Gemara, consisting of legal and nonlegal material; compiled from the Oral Torah and committed to writing between 200–500 C.E.

Talmudim: Students, disciples.

TaNaKh: Acronym for the Hebrew Bible traditionally arranged in the following three sections: (1) Torah (Ta), the Law or the five books of Moses; (2) Nava'im (Na), the Prophets; and (3) Khetuvim (Kh), the Writings. The TaNaKh is also known as the Old

Testament, albeit ordered after the Septuagint (the Greek translation of the Hebrew Scriptures).

Teshuva: Action-oriented repentance; lit., returning to the ways of ADONAI; fundamental component of Tikkun Olam and restoration of the world.

Tetragrammaton: The four letter, ineffable and sacred Name of G-d; from the Hebrew characters yud, hei, vav, hei, usually transliterated YHVH or YHWH; attribute of grace, love and mercy; Cause of All; cf. Ex. 15.

Tikkun: Cosmic reconfiguration and restoration, especially of the sephirot and the archetypes of creation.

Tikkun Olam: (1) Restoration and reconfiguration of our broken, fallen world; (2) fundamental concept of kabbalsitic philosophy; (3) making straight or putting in order; (4) eschatologically, preparation required for the establishment of the Kingdom of G-d; (5) redemption through teshuva and observance of mitzvot; see Mitzvot, Nitzotzot and Tikkun.

Torah: From the root, yara, meaning teaching, instruction; broadly, the Law; (1) the five books of Moses; (2) the TaNaKh; (3) the entire corpus of rabbinical literature; and (4) the Oral Torah.

Tzaddik: (pl. tzaddikim) (1) Righteous person; legally, one who is found to be innocent before the beit din; (2) Hasidic Rebbe; (3) loosely, a seeker of lost sparks, or nitzotzot.

Yamim Nora'im: The High Holy Days, or Ten Days of Awe between Rosh Hashana/Yom Truwah and Yom Kippur; days of repentance and deep soul searching.

Yara Torah: Lit., teaching; instructing the way of Torah.

YHVH or YHWH: See Tetragrammaton.

Yetzer Hara: The evil inclination; impulse within humankind.

Yetzer ha Tov: The good inclination; impulse within humankind.

Yiddische Neshamah: Jewish soul; see Neshamah.

Yom Truwah: Day of Blowing [the Shofar]; see Rosh Hashana and Shofar.

Zohar: Major Jewish mystical work central to the teachings of Kabbalah, published in the 13th century C.E.; stories and teachings ascribed to the first century mystic, Simeon bar Yochai.

Gilgul: Transmigration

Bibliography—Suggested Reading

Cohen, Abraham. *Everyman's Talmud: The Major Teachings of the Rabbinic Sages.* New York: Schocken, 1995.

Frankel, Ellen. *The Classic Tales: 4000 Years of Jewish Lore.* Northvale: Jason Aronson, Inc., 1989.

Gershom, Yonassan. *Beyond the Ashes: Cases of Reincarnation from the Holocaust.* Virginia Beach: A.R.E. Press, 1992.

— *The Mystical Hebrew Alphabet.* Unpublished, 1986.

— *Jewish Tales of Reincarnation.* Northvale: Jason Aronson, Inc., 1999.

— *Forty-Nine Gates of Light: A Course in Kabbalah*, fourth edition www.lulu.com, 2010.

Ibsen, Henrik. *Peer Gynt.* Eds., Paul Negri and Tom Crawford. Trans., William and Charles Archer (1875). Mineola: Dover, 2003.

— *Peer Gynt: Poetry and the Drama.* Trans., Farquharson R. Sharp. London: Temple Press (J.M. Dent & Sons); New York (E.P. Dutton & Co., Inc.), 1950.

Kaplan, Aryeh. *Bahir: Illumination.* York Beach: Samuel Weiser Inc., 1979.

— *Meditation and Kabbalah.* Northvale: Jason Aronson, Inc., 1995.

— *Sefer Yetzirah—The Book of Creation: In Theory and Practice.* San Francisco: Weiser Books, 1997.

Menzi, Donald Wilder and Zwe Padeh. *The Tree of Life: Chayim Vital's Introduction to the Kabbalah of Isaac Luria.* New York: Arizal Publications, Inc., 2000.

Munk, Michael L. *The Wisdom in the Hebrew Alphabet: The Sacred Letters as a Guide to Jewish Deed and Thought.* Brooklyn: Mesorah, 2007.

Samuel, Gabriella. *The Kabbala Handbook: A Concise Encyclopedia of Terms and Concepts in Jewish Mysticism.* New York: Tarcher/Penguin, 2007.

Stern, David. trans. *The Complete Jewish Bible.* Clarksville: JNTP, 1997.

— *Jewish New Testament Commentary.* Clarksville: JNTP, 1992.

Werblowsky, R.J. Zwi and Geoffrey Wigoder. eds. *The Oxford Dictionary of the Jewish Religion.* Oxford: OUP, 1997.

About the Author

Paul Swehla is a chef who holds degrees in education and theology. As a writer of non-fiction, he has produced texts and articles on topics that include horticulture, theology, philosophy, criminal justice reform and the culinary arts. As a student, Paul sat at the feet of internationally renowned author and teacher of Kabbalah, Rabbi Yonassan Gershom. Paul was ordained by Messianic Rabbi, Dr. Avraham Libertus. Gilgul is Paul's first book of poetry. His second, *The Dystopian Hermit Monk* is forthcoming.

Paul is also an amateur musician who has recorded and produced a solo folk album. He plays and sings in jazz, blues and classic rock bands. He enjoys gardening and horticulture. Paul plans to organize a farm to table cabaret that showcases locally grown, free range and sustainably produced artisan foods.

TIKKUN
PUBLISHING
P.O. Box 51
Decorah, IA 52101

paul@tikkunpublishing.com

The law is tempered by grace.

Proof

Made in the USA
Charleston, SC
08 August 2016